On Your
Plate

Bread

Honor Head

A+

Smart Apple Media

Smart Apple Media
P.O. Box 3263, Mankato, Minnesota 56002

Printed in the United States

Published by arrangement with the Watts Publishing Group Ltd, London.

Created by Taglines
Design: Sumit Charles; Harleen Mehta, Q2A Media
Picture research: Pritika Ghura, Q2A Media

Picture credits
t=top b=bottom c=center l=left r=right m=middle

Cover Images: Shutterstock, istockphoto and dreamstime.
Olga Shelego/ Shutterstock: 4, Juriah Mosin/ Shutterstock: 5, Felinda | Dreamstime.com: 6, Condor 36/ Shutterstock: 7,
Kenneth Chelette/ Shutterstock: 8, Joe Gough/ Shutterstock: 9, Graça Victoria/ Istockphoto: 10, rebvt/ Shutterstock: 11,
William Berry/ Shutterstock: 12mr, Mike Grindley/ Shutterstock: 12bl, hugo chang/ Istockphoto: 12br,
ANNAMARIA SZILAGYI/ Shutterstock: 13, Kharidehal Abhirama Ashwin/ Shutterstock: 14, Q2A Media: 15, Disorderly |
Dreamstime.com: 16, Aragorn | Dreamstime.com: 17, Pierre Janssen/ Istockphoto: 18, luminouslens/ Shutterstock: 19, Dumitrescu
Ciprian-Florin/ Shutterstock: 20, Elena Elisseeva/ Shutterstock: 21.

Library of Congress Cataloging-in-Publication Data

Head, Honor.
  Bread / by Honor Head.
      p. cm. -- (On your plate)
  Includes index.
  Summary: "Provides a basic introduction to different kinds of bread and shows examples of different foods to eat with bread."
--Provided by publisher.
  ISBN 978-1-59920-262-4 (hardcover)
  1. Bread--Juvenile literature. 2. Cookery (Bread)--Juvenile literature. I. Title.
  TX769.H396 2010
  641.8'15--dc22

                                                                                                2008039735

9 8 7 6 5 4 3 2 1

Contents

What is bread?

Bread is made from flour. Grains of wheat are ground to make flour.

Golden wheat grows in huge fields.

The flour is mixed with water to make dough. Then yeast is added to make the dough rise.

dough

flour

 The dough is rolled into a ball and baked in the oven.

5

White Bread

White bread is made with flour that uses only a small part of the wheat grain.

crust

The outside of bread is called the crust.

Bread is very good for you.
It gives you lots
of energy.

Eating a
sandwich is a
healthy way to
eat bread.

Wheat Bread

Wheat bread is made with flour that uses a part of the wheat grain called bran.

 Wheat bread is darker than white bread.

Try beans on toast for something different.

Bread can be toasted to make it crispy and crunchy.

Pita Bread

Pita is a flat bread. It can be cut open to make a pita pocket.

A pita pocket can be stuffed with tuna salad and lettuce.

Pitas can be toasted and sliced to make pita wedges.

Crispy pita wedges with dip are good to share with friends.

Rolls and Buns

Rolls are made from different types of dough. Rolls can be cut in half and filled with meat or cheese.

Bagels are great with cream cheese.

dinner roll

bagel

brown roll

12

Hamburgers and hotdogs are eaten on buns.

 A bun filled with a hamburger and toppings is a tasty meal.

Indian Bread

In India, flat bread is used to scoop up food instead of a fork or spoon.

bowls of curry

puri

 Some Indian meals are served with bowls of curry and bread called puri.

Some naans are filled with sweet foods such as coconuts and grapes.

Naans are flat breads. They can be stuffed with meat and vegetables.

Croissants

Croissants come from France. They are soft and flaky.

 Croissants are shaped like a crescent moon.

Some people eat a croissant for breakfast with butter and jelly.

 Croissants can be also be eaten with ham, tomato, and lettuce as a sandwich.

French Bread

French bread is a long, thin loaf of bread. It has a thick, crispy crust.

French bread is soft and chewy on the inside.

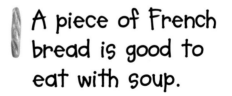 A piece of French bread is good to eat with soup.

It's fun to break apart bread and dip pieces of it into soup.

19

Pizza

The bottom of a pizza is made with the same dough that is used to make bread.

 Toppings such as meats and vegetables can be added to pizza.

A pizza is cooked in an oven. It can be eaten as a main meal with salad.

A slice of pizza is quick and easy to eat.

21

Things to Do

Bread Basket

Can you remember what these breads are called?
Which one is French bread? Wheat bread?
Where are the dinner rolls?

Match Maker!

Can you match the two halves to find a pizza, a bagel, and a croissant?

Make a Meal!

Choose the bread to go with the meal below.

a)   Try me with a bowl of soup.
b)   I am stuffed with tuna salad and lettuce.
c)   Eat me with spicy curry.

23

Glossary

bran
The part of the wheat grain that is nutritious.

curry
A spicy dish that comes from India.

grains
Seeds found at the top of a wheat stalk.

ground
When grains are crushed and made into flour.

rise
When yeast makes the dough get bigger.

Index